52 Days

Ben Wright

52 Days

ISBN-13: 978-0-9888778-9-4
ISBN-10: 0-9888778-9-9

Book Website
www.enwrightened.com

Dedicated To:

My wife Emilee, daughter Brilee and son Graham.

May you continually find God to be your fortress.

Acknowledgements

This book truly could not have been possible without the work of some dear family and friends. I would like to take a moment and thank:

Christy Money, Tim Dooley, and David and Paula Wright

Contents

1. Walls- 15
2. History- 23
3. Tools- 34
4. Rubble- 44
5. Team- 54
6. Construction- 64
7. Victory- 74

Foreword

    The auditorium was at capacity for the Wednesday night keynote lecture. The topic of the lesson was "The Just Shall Live By Faith", from Habakkuk 2:4. The speaker had endured some well-documented hardships in the years preceding this particular lesson and the cold February night was filled with a deafening silence when he spoke the first words of the sermon asking, "Have you ever carried the burden of a broken heart?" As I sat among the crowd that evening and considered what the preacher had been through and how he had endured, how I too and every person in ear shot of the question had faced so many hardships, the consequences of our own sins and the sins of others, the answer to this hypothetical, yet profound, question was an unequivocal "Yes."

    Yes, everyone, at some point will be broken by life! Sin separates us from God (Isaiah 59:1–2). Sin brings death (Romans 5:12). And since all have sinned and continue to fall short of the glory of God (Romans 3:23), all will be broken, defenseless, and vulnerable to the continued attacks of Satan. However, God's love for us and His grief over the plight of His children caused Him to spring into action in order to provide for us, not only salvation from sin and death, but for every spiritual need which enables us to rebuild and defend our lives. The sad fact is that only a few have truly availed themselves of these gifts.

Nehemiah was concerned about the condition of the walls of Jerusalem and carried the burden of a broken heart into the king's presence. He summoned the courage to lead the charge in rebuilding those walls with wisdom, courage, and determination. The amazing feat took only 52 days to complete in spite of the overwhelming magnitude of the job and in the face of intense opposition. Building on this story, Ben weaves together a convincing and convicting parallel to the need most men have today to rebuild their spiritual walls. Ben points out, "Imagine what God can do with you in 52 days if you work hard and let God do His part. He can make you into something you never thought you could be."

This book is masterful in its simplicity and application. The author boldly, yet lovingly, makes some very pointed statements that will make you think and, if you are honest, will move the reader to do something about their spiritual condition. This book is for everybody and the principles laid forth in it are as needed in our culture today as they ever have been. This book will be great for personal/devotional study, family devotionals; it will be a great Bible Class book for teens and adults, and it will be a blessing in sermon preparation and application of the book of Nehemiah.

Ben is my brother in Christ and he is my friend. He is the man I wish I had been when I was a young husband, father, and minister. He has an incredible passion for souls and love for the truth of God's Word. He is also an amazing communicator and writer. This volume is evidence of all that and will bless the reader as it has blessed me. I'm not sure why he asked me to write this foreword, but I am thankful that he did, and I appreciate him, his friendship, and his encouragement more than I could ever express.

Whether your entire wall lies in ruin or simply has been breached by the sins that "so easily ensnare us" (Hebrews 12:1), let us "rise up and build" and let us set our "hands to this good work" (Nehemiah 2:18): the work of rebuilding our spiritual walls. Be faithful!

Timothy L. Dooley
Hebron Kentucky

1

Walls

Imagine a world in which 1600 Pennsylvania Ave NW, Washington, D.C. ceases to exist. The crumbled remains of it are all that are left. The once pristine landscape is now unkempt. Pieces of fighter jets are strewn throughout. Holes in the ground are still visible from where brave soldiers yielded weapons of war to defend the freedom and honor of a mighty country. But they lost. America was defeated. Left without any defenses: No planes. No tanks. No missiles. America unprotected. Exposed. No one is coming to the rescue. Consider what it would feel like to live in a country that at any moment could be invaded.

That scenario feels impossible; but I imagine it felt like that to all once dominate civilizations. Few nations believe they can be conquered, much less decimated. In our times, this would mean disabling aircraft, tanks, and weapons. However, in the times of Nehemiah, it meant tearing down the walls.

Physical Walls

Walls played a significant role in history throughout the Bible. Walls were crucial in the defenses of a city. Nothing was more repellent to an enemy than a well built wall. When the Israelites first attempted to enter the promised land it ended in disaster. The spies reported that the enemies were strong and their cities greatly fortified (Numbers 13:28). Walled cities combined with people described as giants (Numbers 13: 32), led the majority of the spies to conclude that the task of taking the promised land could not be done (Numbers 13:31).

Yet, nearly forty years later, under the leadership of Joshua, what was the first city to be conquered in the promised land? The great walled city of Jericho (Joshua 6). This was no accident. God knew the impact of such a defeat. He knew it would send a message to all nations thereafter: God is mightier than your walls. The people felt safe inside the walls. When they learned of the coming of the Israelites, the first thing they did was shut themselves inside their walls (Joshua 6:1). Nothing in. Nothing out.

God could have defeated the city by any means. He could have created a hole in the wall and allowed the Israelites to pass through it into the city. He could have made stairs to allow them entrance onto the wall. There are dozens of ways God could have allowed the Israelites to enter Jericho. God chose to tear the walls down flat (Joshua 6:20). Why? Domination. If you wanted to dominate, humiliate, and show the world how defeated a city was, you tore down its walls. The rubble was a reminder to the world that the city was broken, vanquished, and no longer a threat. When the walls crumbled, so did the city.

It is understandable, then, when Nehemiah goes to examine the city that he loved that he told the leaders, *"Come, let us rebuild the wall of Jerusalem so that we will no longer be a reproach."* (Nehemiah 2:17). For over a hundred years, though the children of Israel had rebuilt the temple and been allowed to return to Jerusalem, they were an embarrassment. They were a city without walls, susceptible and exposed to all the elements of the outside world. Embarrassing. Disgraceful. Nehemiah knew if the city was to ever be restored, the walls had to be rebuilt.

Spiritual Walls

Walls today in military security are of little value. A wall will no longer protect our nation from military conquest, but God desires to build a spiritual wall around your life and it's more important than most people realize.

One of the verses in the Bible that I have found frightening over the years is Ephesians 6:11-12:

> *"Put on the whole armor of God, that you may be able to stand against the schemes of the devil. For we do not wrestle against flesh and blood, but against the rulers, against the authorities, against the cosmic powers over this present darkness, against the spiritual forces of evil in the heavenly places."*

We are at war. Whether we desire to be or not, we are in a battle. We are fighting an enemy that we neither see, nor fully comprehend. There is an entire army of evil spiritual forces in a realm we have never seen, contending for our souls. An enemy that is happy for us to live our lives in an unfortified city of sinfulness. William Hendrickson, in his *New Testament Commentary on Galatians, Ephesians, Philippians, Colossians and Philemon*, aptly said:

> "The reason for the urgent character of the admonition is that we are not fighting against "flesh and blood," that is, against mere, frail men (Gal. 1:16), with all their physical and mental infirmities (respectively 1 Cor. 15:50 and Matt. 16:17). On the contrary it is against an innumerable super-mundane host of evil spirits: the devil himself and all the demons under his control, that we are waging warfare."

My greatest concern for Christianity today has little to do with political, social, or economic issues, but that so many

Christians are ignorant, that we are at war and, therefore, have no spiritual walls.

God has provided us with the armor necessary to defend ourselves (Ephesians 6: 10-17). The best defense is not only armor, but spiritual fortification inside the refuge of God. Through our obedience to His word, He will build a spiritual wall around our lives. God's desire in this war is to see you truly believe *"God is my Fortress!"* (Psalm 18:2, 31:2-3,46:7, 46:11, 48:3, 59:9,16-17, Psalm 62:2) Without these spiritual walls you are living a life outside the safety of God's stronghold. You are exposed, broken, and barren.

I'm not suggesting that inside this God-built fortress you will never be attacked. It's just the opposite. No one lives in a fortress if they aren't trying to protect themselves. You will be attacked. No question about it. The question is: are you protected? Most all of us would say "yes". We would stand up and shout that God is our refuge and our strength, but our lives tell a different story. It's only a symbolic cry. We like the way it sounds, but we don't like the way it feels to live it. Day after day, if we are being honest, we try to fight this war by our own strength. We are not strong enough. We strategize ways to protect ourselves on our own. We are not crafty enough.

We want all the benefits of the wall, but we don't want the wall. Here's why: walls are restrictive. Walls serve two main purposes: to keep things out, and to keep things in. Those with children understand the benefit of having a fenced yard. It keeps unwanted guests (of various species) from entering your territory unannounced, but it also keeps children safely within clear boundaries. The fence tells anyone that passes by: this land belongs to me. It is universally recognized as a sign to keep out without authorized access. Spiritual walls are no different. When we allow God to build these walls in our lives, it means some things must stay in and some things must always stay out.

Walls are every bit as restrictive as they are protective. We don't like this. We don't want to be told what we can and cannot do or where we can and cannot go. We want limitless freedom, but we desire to be protected. We want to roam freely around outside the walls that God has set until we get hurt or until the world shoves us down. Then we want to turn and run into the protection of God, only to discover that there are restrictions in His protection. So we leave again and the cycle continues.

Building spiritual fortification begins with a commitment to stay within the walls. When we step outside God's refuge, it's a sign to the world that we are exposed and weak. If our lives are a constant cycle between repentance and sinning, perhaps it is because we have not stayed within the fortress. The enemy within the walls is often far more dangerous than those outside. We are our own worst enemy when it comes to breaking down the walls.

In the Garden of Eden, Adam and Eve didn't need a fortress. There was no battle, no sin, but God still built a spiritual wall around them: "And the Lord God commanded the man, saying, *"You may surely eat of every tree of the garden, but of the tree of the knowledge of good and evil you shall not eat, for in the day that you eat of it you shall surely die."* (Genesis 2:16). God offered them freedom, *"you can eat of any tree"* and protection, (don't eat, and you will live). Their protection came at a cost: restriction, *"You shall not eat".* As long as Adam and Eve stayed within the walls God had built around them, they were protected; outside the walls, they died.

When Noah was found to be the only person alive who *"found favor in the eyes of the Lord"* (Genesis 6:8), God gave Him protection: the ark. He gave Him freedom in the form of salvation for his family. That protection came at cost: restriction. Noah had to stay within the physical walls of the ark or he died. The only way Noah stayed within the grace of God was when he committed to staying in the walls, safe in the refuge God had made him.

When Moses led the people out of Egyptian captivity, he gave them the freedom of finally being a people under God. In doing so, God fulfilled a promise He made to Abraham in making them their own special nation (Genesis 12). He gave them protection from their enemies through a standard by which to build their spiritual walls. It consisted of 613 commandments found from Exodus to Deuteronomy. 248 of those commandments were positive commands like, *"You shall love the Lord your God with all your heart and with all your soul and with all your might."* (Deuteronomy 6:5) The other 365 commands were negative commands like, *"You shall not take the name of the Lord your God in vain..."* (Exodus 20:7). These Laws regulated everything the Jews did, from what they ate to how they worshipped, but they served one purpose: protection. The reason they were God's chosen people was because it was through them that God would raise up Jesus. In order to do so, the line of heritage had to be kept pure in order to fulfill God's promise to Abraham. So, God built a wall around them. When they obeyed the Laws they found both spiritual and physical protection (Joshua 1:1-9). When they disobeyed and stepped outside the wall, they died; both spiritually and physically.

When we meet Nehemiah, the last of the great leaders of Israel, he is dealing with a nation that has torn down their walls. Their physical walls were torn down because they had torn down their spiritual walls first. They had let things in which God had told them to keep out, and were a nation in ruin because of it. A nation that had depended upon itself to fight its battles and forgotten what it was like inside the fortress of God. Nehemiah knew that re-building the physical wall of Jerusalem was imperative, but he also knew it would take the rebuilding of their spiritual walls for them to stay rebuilt.

Today, most seem to think that, because we have a better Law under Jesus (Hebrews 10), and because Jesus came to bring *"grace upon grace"* (John 1:16), that we are free to act however we want. While we no longer live under the 615 laws of Moses, does that mean that God will just allow us to do whatever we want? The Bible answers that question for us in Romans 6:15: *"What then? Are we to sin because we are not under law but under grace? By no means!"*

Grace doesn't exist so you can live a life without walls. Jesus didn't die so you could live life however you wanted. The New

Testament, though different from the Old, still contains commands that allow God to build walls around our lives. Again, this law contains both positive and negative commands. It's a spiritual wall. It's restrictive. It keeps things out and keeps things in.

Many today have torn down these walls. Christianity, in general, has decided the walls are no longer necessary. We couldn't be more wrong. We need spiritual walls in our lives. We need to want spiritual walls in our lives. God doesn't tell us not to do things because He's some kind of over-powerful, control freak. He builds these walls for our protection. He knows the enemy. He knows the battle. He builds the walls. In the war being waged for our soul, there is no place I'd rather be than in the fortress of my Savior and King. Begin the process of rebuilding your spiritual walls with a commitment to stay inside the fortifications God has provided.

2

History

There is nothing wrong with being comfortable. In fact, I have invested good money for the sake of being such, into mattresses, couches, even vacations. I have a certain standard of comfort I look for in hotels, restaurants and even at home. Comfort is why I love Snuggies and hate wicker furniture. Given the choice between being comfortable and being uncomfortable, I will always choose comfort.

When we first meet Nehemiah in Nehemiah 1:1, here is what the Bible says about him: *"The words of Nehemiah the son of Hacaliah. Now it happened in the month of Chislev, in the twentieth year, as I was in Susa the citadel,"*. Nehemiah, in the high position of cupbearer to the king, is hanging out in the palace. I've never lived in a palace, but I imagine it to be fairly wonderful, even if you were working there. Nehemiah is content, has a great job, is well respected, well-fed, well-connected, and has a great place to live. By all standards, Nehemiah is comfortable.

As I read the Bible, I find God is not particularly concerned with my comfort level. In fact, He asks me to do some things that, frankly, make me uncomfortable to even think about, much less do. In rebuilding our spiritual walls, we have to understand that this process will make us uncomfortable, or rather, it should make us uncomfortable. Rebuilding our spiritual walls is going to make us live in a way that will not allow us to be comfortable for long.

I don't mean to suggest this new life won't be joyful or happy, but I do need you to know as we start this journey, it's going to take you stepping outside of the plush palace and doing things that sometimes turn your stomach. The only way that Nehemiah ever goes from being comfortable to uncomfortable is if he chooses to. He chose to give up the comforts of a plush life for a commitment to God. That meant going from a life of comfort to a life of being uncomfortable. Not an easy choice to make.

The same is true for you. You have to choose to be uncomfortable. Doing things like praying for your enemy (Matthew 5:44), feeding those who are in need (Matthew 25:31-46), challenging those who are teaching false doctrines (2 Timothy 4:3-5), not worrying (Matthew 6:25-34), putting God's kingdom first (Matthew 6:33), and being ridiculed for following Christ (Matthew 5:11). All of these things are easy to talk about and hard to do. They're hard to do because they make us do things that we are not used to.

Nehemiah chose to leave the comforts of the palace when he learned about the shape of the nation. He chose to give up the comforts of his life in order to fulfill the commitment to His God. God expects the same of us. One of the things that makes us most uncomfortable in this life is remembering our past. Most of us try to move on from and forget our past. This is not a bad thing, by any means, but our past, no matter how bad it is, has shaped who we are today and, therefore, is important to us rebuilding our walls. There is a lot of value in history, if we are willing to face it with honesty and through the correct lenses.

How Did I Get Here?

I love the story of Nehemiah. I love it because it's a victory; a glorious, wonderful achievement of what happens when human will lets down their own selfish pretense, submits their will to God's will, and works together for a single cause. In 52 days, Nehemiah led a group of people to rebuild the walls of Jerusalem; something that hadn't been done in the previous years before him. However, before we can ever rebuild the walls in our lives, we must first ask a question that is tough: Why was the wall torn down in the first place?

Nehemiah answers this question in a prayer. *"We have acted very corruptly against you and have not kept the commandments, the statutes, and the rules that you commanded your servant Moses. Remember the word that you commanded your servant Moses, saying, 'If you are unfaithful, I will scatter you among the peoples."* (Nehemiah 1:7-8). The city and the people were in ruins because they had failed to keep the commandments of God. That part is straightforward. The walls fell because of disobedience, but it's more complicated and tragic than Nehemiah tells in that passage. The history of just why they were standing in rubble is one of the most heartbreaking, awful, dreadful stories in existence. Before we rebuild our walls, we must first understand, in detail, why they went from glorious to grotesque.

It goes back hundreds of years before Nehemiah was ever even thought of, back before the walls of Jerusalem were even built. In the genesis of the great Israelite nation, God issued them many warnings concerning the punishment for disobedience. Some of those "curses" are pretty hard to take in, even today. For example, in Deuteronomy 28:15-19, God told them this:

> *"But if you will not obey the voice of the Lord your God or be careful to do all His commandments and His statutes that I command you today, then all these curses shall come upon you and overtake you. Cursed shall you be in the city, and cursed shall you be in the field.*

25

Cursed shall be your basket and your kneading bowl. Cursed shall be the fruit of your womb and the fruit of your ground, the increase of your herds and the young of your flock. Cursed shall you be when you come in, and cursed shall you be when you go out."

God's rule was pretty simple: stay within the spiritual walls I have set, and you will be blessed. Leave the spiritual walls or tear them down, and I will no longer protect you. The word "cursed" sounds pretty harsh in and of itself, but in Deuteronomy 28: 49-57 we get all the gritty details of the curse. Here are some of the highlights:

• God would send a nation against them, that spoke a language they wouldn't understand (Deuteronomy 28:49).

• This nation would destroy their crops, livestock, and food supplies (Deuteronomy 28:51).

• This nation would take all their towns and destroy their walls (Deuteronomy 28:52).

• During the siege of Jerusalem, the famine would get so bad, that even the respectable men would start eating their own children. Not only that, but they would do it in secret as to not have to share. The women would eat their afterbirth from having children (Deuteronomy 28:53-55).

How hungry would you have to be to even consider eating your own children? It is a terrible thought. It seems ludicrous. Surely this would never happen. When the town of Samaria was under siege from Ben-Hadad King of Syria, in 2 Kings 6, there was a famine so great that people started eating donkey's heads and dove feces, (2 Kings 6:25). Worse than that, they actually ate another human being, with intentions of eating more than one (2 Kings 6:26-30). This siege was far shorter and less fierce than the one Jerusalem would endure. Can you imagine what happened in Jerusalem?

Your past may not have cannibalism in it, but it might be equally as terrifying. If you cringe when you think about your past mistakes, I need you to know you are not alone in this. I know very few people who have lived without doing a few things they regret. These past memories can be terrifyingly painful, and chances are you've locked them away for years, praying that no one finds out about your past.

Here's the thing I think we miss: even if your past is bad, you can use it for good. Every mistake you have made in the past is a result of poor decisions. Whether we like it or not, we have chosen, through a series of both minor and major choices, where we are today. While we may have chosen poorly in the past, we can use this knowledge of our history to avoid such decisions in the future

.

Questions That Hurt

How do we do that? It starts with a simple concept: ask questions that hurt. In the case of Nehemiah, it looked like this, *"And I asked them concerning the Jews who escaped, who had survived the exile, and concerning Jerusalem"* (Nehemiah 1:2). Upon seeing some of his brothers return from Jerusalem, Nehemiah asked some questions that he didn't have to ask: "How are the Jews doing? What's the status of Jerusalem's rebuild?"

If Nehemiah never inquired about the city, he would have been none the wiser to its status. Nehemiah could have chosen just to ignore it. He could have chosen to simply go about his life, unconcerned with those who weren't concerned with him. After all, Nehemiah had never lived in Jerusalem. He had never seen the glorious temple of Solomon and, to the best of my knowledge, had never seen the city. Yet, he did ask.

It was a question that hurt because it changed his accountability. He went from someone with credible ignorance to someone who was now in the know about the poor condition of his city. He went from being blissfully uninformed to guiltily learned. By asking this question, he could no longer lay his head down at night without knowing that the city of his heritage was desolate. Asking the question changed his life.

We need questions that hurt, and God asks them. He asks

the questions that cause us to go from oblivious to informed. In our journey to build our spiritual walls, these questions begin with ourselves. We must first ask ourselves how we got here and why our spiritual wall is the way that it is. Is it torn down? Built up? On fire? Non-existent? Halfway done? A glorious fortress of wonder? Are you saved? Lost? Don't know? Don't Care?

We must ask ourselves the questions, to which only we will know the answers. Often, we know these questions exist in our mind, but we are afraid to ask them. We are afraid because they hurt. We are afraid because once we ask them, we are accountable for their answers. It's time to stop being afraid. Ask yourself the question that needs to be asked, but don't stop there.

Answers That Hurt

Sometimes, truth is a brutal thing. Truth tears down the fantasies that we often live in and snaps us instantly back to reality. Perhaps, that's why we have gone the way of sugar-coating things. Kids are no longer told they lost, but are given "participation trophies". You no longer fail a class, you "didn't meet the academic expectations of the course". I'm not sure either of those things has made the world a better place. Asking questions that hurt generally leads to answers that hurt, as well.

Nehemiah asked questions he didn't have to ask. He could have remained blissfully unaware of the status of Jerusalem, but he chose to ask them. By asking the question, Nehemiah must now be prepared to hear the truth; a truth that would hurt. Here is the answer he received concerning his question: *"And they said to me, The remnant there in the province who had survived the exile is in great trouble and shame. The wall of Jerusalem is broken down, and its gates are destroyed by fire."* (Nehemiah 1:3)

Judging by his reaction, this must have been a shock to Nehemiah. It broke his heart and moved him to tears. It was the best thing that ever happened to him. Nehemiah needed an answer that hurt. He needed to know the condition of the city, or else he never would have instituted the changes that were needed.

Hanani and the other men didn't have to give him such an answer. They could have lied and reasoned that there was nothing Nehemiah could do anyway. They could have sugar-coated it and said, "Well, you know they aren't doing as well as they should but we think they will bounce right back." None of those would have been beneficial to Nehemiah. He needed tough answers to tough questions.

God is not afraid to ask tough questions. He, also, is not afraid to give tough answers. These answers hurt. They hurt because it's what you need but don't want to hear. You still need to hear them. The tough part about the questions we are asking in this book is that you have no one to answer them for you. Your closest friend, parent, or spouse probably doesn't know the conditions of your spiritual walls. You know the state of your walls. You know the condition of your soul.

At this point, you really have two choices in the matter: you can continue to lie to yourself about the condition of your walls, or you can finally be honest with yourself. If you are going to choose the first, then by all means, put this book down and go watch TV. Today is the day you have to start being honest with yourself.

Stop sugar coating the truth about your soul. Only you know what it is, but you have to face the reality of its condition. It is only when you decide to be honest with yourself that you can begin to repair the damage. It's going to hurt, or at least it should. If your walls are in disrepair, facing the truth about them is exactly what you need to hear.

Weeping and Mourning
I can only think of a few times in my life I have wept uncontrollably. Once, during the death of my Grandmother, once following the birth of my daughter, and once while watching "Marley and Me", (don't act like you didn't cry, too). It's a miserable feeling to mourn and weep, but it's a necessary part of the grieving process.

After asking the tough questions and getting a brutally honest answer, here is what Nehemiah's reaction was, *"As soon as I heard these words I sat down and wept and mourned for days..."* (Nehemiah 1:4). Weeping and mourning for days. That was Nehemiah's reaction to the news that the people and city he loved were in disrepair. Let that sink in for a moment. Nehemiah didn't know most of these people personally. Yet when he heard the news, he wept and mourned for days. If Nehemiah had this kind of a reaction to bricks, mortar, and strangers being broken, how should we respond when we are broken?

We need more weeping and mourning in our world today, not pity parties, not self-loathing, but serious heart-brokenness over the spiritual condition of our lives. If your walls are broken and you don't feel bad about it, you have a problem. When you answered those questions about your spiritual condition, you should have been distraught if it wasn't where it should be. You should be weeping and mourning if God is not your refuge and if your soul is lost.

We are all broken. Our walls from time to time are torn down, and sin seeps into our life and sets up camp. We should feel bad about it. We should weep and mourn for it because it means that we care. It means our heart has not been hardened beyond repair. When your walls are broken and you no longer weep and mourn, you have a heart that has been calloused over. A heart that has been taught to stop feeling is a great weapon of the Enemy in our spiritual war. When we stop feeling guilty for breaking our spiritual walls, Satan is winning and we don't even know it.

Perhaps, you aren't the weeping and mourning type. I get it. Not everyone grieves the same and that's fine. You may not shed a tear over this because you don't shed tears for anything. You can still grieve. Your heart needs to break, whether your tear ducts do or not.

This part is scary because it makes us vulnerable. It makes us realize we are broken and that we are in need of repair. This is not a bad thing. Weeping and mourning does not make you weak.

It makes you wise. You need to experience the heart breaking before you can be in repair.

Praying For Success

Nehemiah doesn't just weep and mourn for days upon end, feeling sorry for the nation of Israel. He starts in the most powerful place he knows: prayer. Prayer is the single-most potent defense we have against any enemy. It's the most comforting, as well. I find Nehemiah's prayer to be fascinating.

> *"And I said, O Lord God of heaven, the great and awesome God who keeps covenant and steadfast love with those who love him and keep his commandments, let your ear be attentive and your eyes open, to hear the prayer of your servant that I now pray before you day and night for the people of Israel your servants, confessing the sins of the people of Israel, which we have sinned against you. Even I and my father's house have sinned. We have acted very corruptly against you and have not kept the commandments, the statutes, and the rules that you commanded your servant Moses. Remember the word that you commanded your servant Moses, saying, 'If you are unfaithful, I will scatter you among the peoples, but if you return to me and keep my commandments and do them, though your outcasts are in the uttermost parts of heaven, from there I will gather them and bring them to the place that I have chosen, to make my name dwell there.' They are your servants and your people, whom you have redeemed by your great power and by your strong hand. O Lord, let your ear be attentive to the prayer of your servant, and to the prayer of your servants who delight to fear your name, and give success to your servant today, and grant him mercy in the sight of this man."*

I love the last part. Nehemiah confidently and directly tells God he needs a few things to succeed at building the wall. The one I find most telling is that he asks God to help him succeed. Such a subtle, but often overlooked, idea.

Perhaps we fail more often than not because we do not ask

God to allow us to succeed. I'm not sure why we don't ask more often. I've heard prayers along the lines of "help us to succeed if it's what you want, and help us to fail if it's not" before, but that's not what Nehemiah does. He prays with confidence, *"give me success"*.

James said, in the New Testament, that we are to pray with confidence (James 1:6). Too often, we do not receive things because we've never asked God for them. In every endeavor we choose to partake in, but especially in the rebuilding of our walls, let us pray to God for success in doing so. He blessed Nehemiah and He will do the same for us.

History in the Making

Let's take our new found inventory of our life and use it for our good. Your past is your past, but it also has helped define who you are. You can use that past to make your future history a better history. Nehemiah was fully aware of the haunted past of his people. They certainly weren't proud of what they had become, but Nehemiah used this as a springboard for building a motivation for constructing better walls. You can do the same.

Use your past to build up spiritual defenses in the places you know you need them the most. Today, let's mourn our past and celebrate our future.

3

Tools

Every once in a while, I get the feeling that I need to build something. This feeling has occasionally crept up on me since I was a kid. When I was a child, that outlet was usually a beautiful masterpiece of blocks. As an adult, I found myself drawn to build bigger things. Not too long ago, my wife and I were searching for a dining room table for our new home. We both knew what we wanted: an adequately sized farm-house table. So we did some research and found the ideal table for us. The problem was, it was really expensive. Since we couldn't justify the cost, I decided I would build the table. I had never built anything significant in my life and soon discovered I needed some new tools. Once I had the proper tools, the job was much easier and I was able to do it with relative ease.

In rebuilding our spiritual walls, we need to have the proper tools for the job. Without them, we will be at a severe disadvantage. The good news is that most possess the tools necessary to do this, they just need to learn to harness them properly.

Resources of the King

Tools are extremely expensive. They cost a lot of money to purchase and to own. Some are even so expensive that they need to be rented, rather than purchased. If you are anything like me, your resources for such tools are extremely limited. From time to time, I'll watch a home renovation show where they will transform these homes that are atrocious into something that looks like it came out of a magazine - and they do it in one day. It always leaves me with the feeling that "hey, I could do that, too". It only took me one shower remodel to realize that those people have the full resources of a television network behind them. They have the best people and the best tools because they have the proper resources.

Rebuilding our spiritual walls is going to be expensive. I'm warning you in advance so that you will be prepared. I'm not sure who started the complacent movement that being a Christian is free. It isn't. A religion that doesn't cost anything isn't worth anything. It violates the basic principles of sowing and reaping (Galatians 6:7). It also violates every notion of following Jesus (Luke 9:23-24). The process of rebuilding your spiritual walls shouldn't cost something; it *must* cost something.

Nehemiah recognizes this fact almost immediately. He knows the process of rebuilding the walls of Jerusalem will be very expensive, and not just in terms of money. It's going to take tools, resources, people, authority, and time. Nehemiah knows in his heart that he can't do this on his own. He doesn't have the tools to do the job. All the confidence and can-do attitude in the world is useless without the necessary resources. This monumental task of rebuilding the walls was going to take the resources of a king. That's exactly where you'll find Nehemiah starting (Nehemiah 2). Nehemiah first seeks the proper tools from a place where he knows he has virtually limitless resources.

I've often wondered what I could accomplish if money were no object; if I had access to every tool that I would need. I'll probably never find out, but I do know this: in my efforts to build spiritual walls, I need access to the resources of a King. I think it's easy for us to forget sometimes that the Christian life we are building isn't dependent upon our own resourcefulness. I am weak, without authority, and broke, but my King isn't. He has untold riches, limitless resources, and a willingness to allow me to tap into those things. We're going to talk about the tools we need to rebuild our walls, but first, I need you to understand it will be impossible without the riches of God backing you. You must ask for these resources and be confident God will give them to you, (James 1:6).

Tool #1: Respect

I find how God's people addressed royalty in the Bible to be fascinating, especially in light of how the world treats political leaders today. Not a single day goes by that I don't see someone on social media bash the President or a politician. Yet, when I look at the Bible I see that, generally speaking, God's people were respectful of those who were put in charge, even when they didn't have the same moral values. Nehemiah is no exception to this. I'm sure he and King Artaxerxes had very different world views, yet they seemed to be able to coexist peacefully and work together. Why? Respect.

Nehemiah's respect for King Artaxerxes is evident by the way he approaches the precarious situation of wanting to rebuild the walls of Jerusalem. Nehemiah doesn't march in and demand to be sent there. He doesn't bash the King in ancient scrolls about how he's let his city lie in ruins. In fact, Nehemiah doesn't even want the King to know he is sad, (Nehemiah 2:2). Notice, though, how he addresses the King, respectfully, when asked what was ailing him (Nehemiah 2:3). Their respect was a two-way street. Nehemiah knew Artaxerxes was his superior on this earth and he treated him that way. Because the proper respect was shown, Nehemiah was privileged to be in a position where his wishes could be met. He had earned the respect of the King. His respect for the King stemmed from his higher respect for his God.

Respect for God seems to be a lost art today. I bet more blasphemous, disrespectful things have been said about God via the media in the last 10 years than all previous generations combined. There has never been a time when respect for God was more needed. The phrase "fear God" or "fear of the Lord" is found more than 40 times throughout the Bible and greatly suggests the Lord is deserving of a healthy dose of respect.

One of my favorite Bible stories is found in Mark 5. Jesus gets out of a boat and is met by this demon possessed man. The man is naked, has been cutting himself with stones, living in a graveyard, and has super-human strength. This is one scary dude. In fact, we will learn later in the story that this man has multiple demons possessing him. When you think demons, you probably have a pop culture idea of demons. Peoples' heads spinning around, puking pea soup, and generally blaspheming the name of God by cursing Him. Yet, this group of demons addresses Jesus, in Mark 5:7: *"And crying out with a loud voice, he said, 'What have you to do with me, Jesus, Son of the Most High God? I adjure you by God, do not torment me.'"* Did you notice how respectful the demons were of Jesus? It is sad to think that demons are often more respectful of our Savior than we are.

The first tool you need in rebuilding your spiritual walls is respect for God. Without this key step, nothing else will matter. If you don't fear the Lord, you will never understand why you're doing what you are doing. Respect starts with getting to know someone. I have no respect for someone that I don't know. Why? Because I don't know them. Nehemiah could respect Artaxerxes because he had a relationship with him. He knew who he was, what he did, and what he stood for. Nehemiah didn't just know facts about Artaxerxes, he had a relationship with him. While they probably weren't best friends, Artaxerxes had enough trust and respect for Nehemiah to make him a cupbearer and entrust him with a very important job.

In order to respect God, you must first know God. You must have a relationship with Him that is so deep, you'll do anything to protect it, (hence, spiritual walls). This relationship will probably start with knowing facts about God. Over time, though, those facts must turn into intimate knowledge and a relationship that's more than just following a set of rules. It must be such that you witness the character of God everyday in your life, and develop such reverence for Him that you can't help but respect Him in every aspect of your life.

This tool is a cornerstone for all the other tools. It will cause us to continually protect what we are going to build up. Respect for God must be the first tool we develop to build our walls.

Tool # 2: Honesty

It's hard to be honest. I'll admit it. I wouldn't call myself a liar, per say, but I have told a few fibs. Notice, I didn't say "lies". I chose "fibs" unintentionally because it was the first word that came to mind. It came to mind first because "lie", frankly, sounded too harsh. I don't lie, I fib. I'm sure you know exactly what I'm talking about. We even lie, err...fib about lying. I'm not sure why we refuse to be more honest. Perhaps it has to do with the consequences of telling the truth. We sometimes lie so much that we don't even think we are lying. Take this small example. Someone says, "How are you today?" 99.9% of the time, what is your response? Fine? Good? Excellent? How often is that true? I've found myself saying it even when I was feeling absolutely miserable. In fact, you'll notice that if you've ever asked someone how they are doing and they respond with something besides fine, you're a little shocked, aren't you?

In Nehemiah 2, Nehemiah was faced with a choice: be honest with the King about what was bothering him and risk being killed, (it was unlawful to be sad in the presence of the King), or lie about it. It would have been a small lie, right? Surely, it would have been justified, right? Put yourself in Nehemiah's shoes and ask what you would have done. However, Nehemiah did what was within his character as a man of God; he told the truth.

It's been my experience that the person I lie to most often

is myself. It's sad, really. I've lied to myself about my talents, abilities, looks, charm, confidence, character, and the list could go on and on. Most often, though, I think that I've lied to myself about my sin.

Human beings have a peculiar way of justifying our actions. We are quick to point out the flaws of others, but rarely realize that our sins are often much bigger. This is exactly the point of what Jesus said about judging, in Matthew 7. He wasn't suggesting it was wrong to call out sin. What He was essentially saying is that you must take care of your own sin before you take care of anyone else's. Taking care of your own sin starts with being honest about it with yourself.

I don't know what your struggle is, but I know that spiritual walls are often broken down from the inside out. They are ripped apart by skeletons we have left hanging in closets, hoping they never come back to life. They always come back to life. When they do, they will rip your spiritual walls apart brick by brick and destroy every spiritual fortification you have worked so hard for. This is what happens when we simply choose to ignore sin in our lives. I'm not sure it can be put any plainer than this, *"But if you will not do so, behold, you have sinned against the Lord, and be sure your sin will find you out,"* (Numbers 32:23).

James said that people who were hearers of the Word and not doers were like people who looked in the mirror and then stepped away and forgot what they looked like (James 1:22-25). I can't tell you how often I've done this in my own life with sin. I've wanted so badly for it not to be there that I have just chosen to ignore it, in hopes that it would go away. It never does. Sin, unaddressed, will haunt you like a bad dream that you can't escape. I'm not talking about "little" sins, (more about this in another chapter), such as "oh, I didn't read my Bible today, or pray today." Those are sins we are willing to openly admit to. I'm talking about the big stuff. The career ruiners, the marriage hurters, the "that's so bad, I'm going to stop being your friend" sins. The ones we don't talk about.

Yet, the Bible speaks clearly on the topic. The way to address these things is not to hide behind them for fear of them being exposed, but to expose them to your brothers and sisters in Christ (James 5:16). You can't do this unless you are honest about them. If you're not going to be honest about what struggles you face or sins you need to take care of, there's no point in rebuilding the walls; they will come down quickly and violently from within. Honesty is a tool you must equip yourself with.

Tool # 3: Time

I'm not a guy who has ever been able to successfully pull off a watch. It always feels awkward, no matter how long I wear it. However, there is one watch that I have probably worn more than any other. It belonged to my grandfather, who died before I was born. He was my dad's father and my dad gave me the watch. The watch has fascinated me because it was the watch that my grandfather wore the day he died. It's just always put things into perspective; how, even after his life was over, the clock kept ticking.

Can I tell you that time is the most valuable commodity in the world today? It's rarer, more expensive, and more valuable than all the gold, silver, and technology in existence. I know this because people are often willing to give money before they will donate their time. Which is easier to convince someone to do: getting someone to commit to giving $20, or getting someone to commit to an hour of time? Time is so precious because it's our most limited resource. They aren't making more of it. You can't buy it, and you can't create. Once time is gone, it's gone. James famously described life as a vapor, here today, gone tomorrow (James 4:14).

We've mentioned already the importance of Nehemiah's job. He's a well-respected individual in the kingdom for which he works. Yet, Nehemiah makes the time to be able to do what was truly important to him. There is no doubt Nehemiah would have been a busy man. There is also little doubt that he could have requested that King Artaxerxes send someone else to do this. However, Nehemiah knew the importance of such a task and what it would mean for him to be involved.

Don't send someone to do a job you should be doing. Perhaps the biggest misstep we have in rebuilding our walls is a failure to dedicate the time to do so. We want to figure out a way to have spiritual fortification with the least amount of invested time possible. We want the abbreviated version of the instruction manual. We ask questions like, "how much do I have to do to please God?" When we should be asking, "What else can I do to please God?" The most important tool on your side today is time.

The problem is, besides being a rare commodity, time is also an unstable one. There is no guarantee of time. Therefore, every single second must be well-thought out and used meticulously for the glory of God. The shape of your spiritual walls will depend mainly on how much time you dedicate to rebuilding them.

Before you go rearranging your schedule, though, let me caution you not to segment your life. People often arrange their lives in chunks of time. I go to school/work for this block of time, I exercise for this block of time, I have family concerns for this block of time, etc. It only comes naturally, then, in this kind of thinking, to segment a time for God. Thinking like this is noble, but faulty. By giving God a time slot, you are essentially putting God in a box and saying, "God, for x-number of minutes a day, I'm all yours", and we limit the influence God can have on our life. Instead of splitting our lives into segments and giving God just a slot, we should be inserting God into each segment. We should be constantly asking ourselves how we can use what we are involved in for the glory of God, (Colossians 3:17).

I hear a lot of talk about priorities and making God first in people's lives. It is, again, a noble idea, but one that I think we must strongly consider the meaning of. God isn't looking for you to give Him a block of time each week. He's looking for you to give Him all of your time each week, in every block. What most people need is not necessarily a reprioritization of their lives, but a change of how they approach every aspect of their life by inserting God into every moment.

When you begin to realize that God is in every aspect of your life, you will then begin to understand the importance of spiritual fortification. You will discover that, when God is consistently a part of your life, you're going to want to have walls that will hold up under any circumstance. This process requires the world's costliest resource: time.

Notice also, Nehemiah gave the King a set time from for accomplishing his goal (Nehemiah 2: 6). He does so because his King asked for it. He knew that he could not be gone forever in this task and must use the time he had wisely. I don't know how long Nehemiah told Artaxerxes he needed to complete the task, but I know he did give him a time. For Nehemiah, the actual process of building the walls took 52 days. Nehemiah had given himself a time limit.

You need a time frame to rebuild your spiritual walls. Trust me, as someone who deals with writers on a daily basis, you need a deadline for this process. Granted, it will be a lifelong work to maintain it, but you need a time frame for rebuilding it. Get your calendar out and mark a date by which you want to see significant spiritual change, then work hard to meet that goal. You must give yourself a deadline to set yourself up for success in completing your goal.

Equipping

There are many other tools that Nehemiah has before he goes into the monumental task of rebuilding these walls. He gets letters of authority to pass through various properties, he gets access to the King's lumber resources, and he receives permission to go. Nehemiah would have all the tools he needed to complete the job. He would have complete access to the resources of a king. What happens if Nehemiah never uses them?

You have all the tools you need, as well. God has given you what you need to make your life a spiritually-fortified one. The question is, will you actually use the tools?

4

Rubble

I remember exactly where I was on September 11, 2001. If you are old enough, you do, too. I was sitting on the stage of our gymnasium at school when I heard about the planes. We all ran to the nearest classroom to watch the news coverage. No one spoke; not even a whisper. Everyone stood in awe. I remember watching replays of the towers crumbling to the ground and the 1,300 feet of building material crashing to earth. I remember the huge cloud of dust it created that seemed to cover everything, like a blizzard of ash. I remember the wreckage of mangled steel beams, wires, and concrete. I remember thinking, "How are they ever going to clean this up?"

Sometimes, I feel the same way about my life. It seems that, every so often, my world just falls apart. It's not random. It's the result of inadequate preparation and poor decisions. Walls don't just fall down by themselves; they have to be forced. When the walls do fall down, though, the mess they leave behind is often far greater than when you had no walls at all.

In Nehemiah 2: 11-17, Nehemiah goes to Jerusalem to examine the remains of the city. He begins to inspect the walls and gates in great detail before he ever even attempts to build a new section of wall. Why did he do this? I mean, realistically, Nehemiah knew the wall was in bad shape, he knew it needed to be rebuilt; why not just bring a whole team of people in immediately and start? Nehemiah knew the importance of evaluation. He knew it was essential to see exactly what kind of rubble he was dealing with.

I don't care for self-examination. I prefer to live in a world where I make no mistakes and everyone loves me for who I am. Unfortunately, it's just not true. I make mistakes and not everyone loves me. Those mistakes have hurt myself and others. However, if we are going to rebuild our spiritual walls, we have to pause here and be brutally honest. What kind of rubble are we dealing with in our lives? Where are the holes in our spiritual fortification? What do we need to remove in order to rebuild? These are all questions we must answer.

Weak Points

As Nehemiah begins his examination of the walls, something interesting happens. He not only takes a look at the wall structure, but spends a considerable amount of time at the gates. You'll notice this pattern later on, as well, during construction. It is my understanding that the gates were the weakest, most suscep- tible, and vulnerable, yet necessary, part of a city's structure. Gates were a necessary evil; people and things had to be able to come in and out to keep the city functioning. They were also a huge liability, often a chink in the armor of even the most impenetrable fortress. Nehemiah knew significant attention must be given to the weakest points.

As we consider the idea of rebuilding our spiritual walls,

we must understand that every person has weak points in their nature. We must live in this world. In the middle of a sin-filled, dark, angry, hate-filled planet we are called to dwell, not just to exist, but to be light, permeating the darkness on all sides. That, whether we like it or not, means that we must interact with the world in some ways. It often means letting things in and out of fortification, but also presents a huge opportunity for us to be vulnerable.

As a result of this, Christians often go to one of two extremes. There are those who recognize these weaknesses and decide to do what they can to live as outside of the world in everyday life as they possibly can. They may not become monks who recluse and live on some mountain in Tibet, but they're not far behind. They want to interact with the world as little as possible, and minimize or eliminate the possibility that a weakness would be exposed. So they withdraw. The problem is, as Christians we are called to interact with the world. We are called to be a part of the social interaction that exists on Earth. You can't save something you aren't a part of. Jesus didn't come to this earth and then hole up in a house the whole time He was here for fear of failing. No, He chose to interact with the world in a manner that drew people to Him.

The opposite end of that is the people who want to be so close to the world that they can't really tell what's holy and what isn't. They take social interaction to the extreme and do not wish to stand out in any way from the world. They want you to see Jesus in a very socially acceptable way; as a friendly, neighborly guy who never frowned or got angry. They have no concerns for their weaknesses because "everybody sins", and "don't judge me for sinning differently than you". And so, this is the state that Christianity is quickly becoming. The idea is that as long as you share your weak points, it's totally fine for them to just be.

Neither of these extremes are what God is looking for. We are called to be people who interact with the world, but we are also called to be different. We are called to be people who are loving and kind, but also people who stand up for the truth. We are to feed the hungry and clothe the poor, but also take care of ourselves. We are called to be cautious of our own sins, but to also look out for the sins of others. We must never forget these truths.

Yet, we also need to be cautious, and understand that each one of us has weaknesses in our spiritual fortification that must be examined and constantly watched. Each person has a struggle, a temptation that is unique to them. These vary in size and extremity, but they do not differ in their power to destroy. What may be easy for you to resist might be devastating to another. It's really the beauty of bearing one another's burdens (Galatians 6:1-3).

We cannot be ignorant of our weaknesses. We must walk the rubble of our walls and find what they are and how they can be fixed. This begins with asking ourselves about our spiritual struggles. What is it in this life that is holding you back from being the kind of person that you claim to want to be? What is the temptation you find most appealing? What struggle do you pray about most often? What sin do you find yourself continually falling into? What are your weaknesses?

This information will come in handy when we start the construction of our new spiritual walls. If you know your own weaknesses, you can begin to assess just what kind of fortification you're going to need.

All Rubble Isn't Equal
I envision the scenes of Nehemiah 2 in my head as he's carefully walking through the once glorious city. In my mind, I can imagine the smell of small fires burning nearby, a distinct smell that I've witnessed in countless numbers of cities which are poor. I can see the dust covering his face as he weaves over stones and looks under rocks. I can feel the heat from the remnants of the wall as they have soaked up the day's sun and as Nehemiah sees all the pieces of the rubble, both great and small.

The thing about rubble is that it comes in all sizes and forms. Some of it is quite easy to pick up and discard, other pieces require more laborious means of removing. It's true with sin, too. As we have discussed in previous chapters, the reason the walls of Jerusalem are torn down all boils down to sin. The same is true for our spiritual walls. The mess that our spiritual life gets in is all a result of sin. So, as we examine the rubble, I think it's important for us to understand that, despite what you've heard, not all sin is equal.

Now before you call me a heretic and break into one of those "sin is sin" speeches, please let me explain. All sin is equal, in the fact that it all breaks the law of God. A lie breaks the law of God, just the same as a murder does, but these two sins are not equal, not by any stretch of the imagination. Allow me to illustrate. You're driving down a road with a speed limit of 55 mph and you are traveling at 59 mph. You get pulled over and receive a ticket for speeding. You might argue and say, "I was just going 4 over", but when it comes down to it, you broke the law, even though the infraction was small. However, let's imagine that you are traveling down that same road with the same speed limit, only this time you are going 90 mph. You get pulled over. You've broken the law just the same as you did when going 4 mph over, but are they equal? Absolutely not. They are only equal in the sense that they both broke the law, but not in terms of consequences.

The same is true of sin. While we could spend a considerable amount of time discussing the issue of varying degrees of punishment and reward in the next life, our time will be mainly focused on the consequences of sin in this one, and they are not all equal. A lie may just as easily violate the law of God as murder, but no one would agree that they are equals. Forgiveness does not equal the resolution of consequences in any way in this life, though it certainly does in the next. In this life, regardless of how many times God or people forgive, you will still have to deal with the retributions of your actions. Some sins even have lifetime consequences that, even after you rebuild your walls, will still have to be dealt with. Some of the sin you are going to be dealing with in cleaning up your spiritual walls will be quite easily removed, but some of it will take years and leave holes the size of boulders. You must carry on and repair it.

The consequence of each sin is different and, therefore, every person's situation is different. Sin always multiplies, which is why it is important to address it as it comes along. For some reading this, you have been gathering rubble and trash for years and years. You've dealt with a number of sins and never properly handled them, and for you to begin to clear the rubble is going to cause a significant amount of pain and agony. Please, hear me on this: you can't build new walls on old rubble. It will cause the walls to be weak and fall even faster than before.

It might be that you need to admit to an addiction, problem or a lie. It might be that you must finally come to grips with the fact that you are struggling with your sexuality. It might be casting out the demons that have haunted you for years in the form of pills, alcohol, anger, violence, grief, gluttony, or worry. It might take you confessing something you have never wished to confess to anyone, ever. It will feel like someone has stabbed you in the gut and keeps turning it around, but you cannot rebuild your walls without first removing the rubble. Trust me. I've been there, through many sleepless nights, wondering how I was going to deal with the actions that had taken place. I've cried and prayed, but eventually, you must confess. You must acknowledge the rubble before it can be removed.

Evaluate with caution and care. The rubble you are going to remove will leave holes that must be filled with something solid, something better. The pain and the grief that you will have will eventually lead to clarity and a clear ground for building something extraordinary.

Burning the Trash

When I was a kid, my mom worked for a company that her parents owned. The office was located just a short walk downhill from my grandmother's house. Needless to say, I spent a lot of time there as a kid, roaming the hills, fishing, and finding other cool things in and around their house and office. There were also a few people, who helped keep up the landscaping, roaming around from time to time. I remember on one occasion, I walked outside to find someone burning trash in a big steel trash can. Being the curious little guy that I was, I decided to inspect this phenomenon closer; but as I approached, a piece of the trash that was burning flew out and landed right on my sandal-clad foot. I remember the searing pain that I felt as the burning ash melted my flesh, (it was much worse in my head). I remember screaming, and even crying a bit, but most of all I remember the guy who was burning the trash, laughing at me as I danced around in pain. I learned a lesson that day that I will never forget: burning the trash is painful, stinky, and dangerous, but absolutely necessary.

The text never mentions anything about Nehemiah burning trash, or even clearing the rubble. I'm making an informed assumption here that it took place, because it had to. At some point, they had to clean up the mess that had been left behind before they could build anything new. Someone had to pick up the stones, someone had to burn the trash, and I'm guessing it's a job that no one wanted.

Some people today are spiritual hoarders. If we had hidden cameras and could peek into their life, we wouldn't find mounds of old catalogs or freezers full of rotten meat. But if we could somehow look into their spiritual life, we would find things that probably couldn't be shown on television. Some have been hoarding terrible spiritual things for years. They've been holding on to grudges, temptations, anger, guilt, worry, denial, and doubt for years and years. They've held on to this these things so long that they are worried about what would happen if they ever had to let them go. They've become the spiritual equivalent of Gollum's ring, "their precious", if you will. Even though it's the thing that's causing them the most pain, they've confused joy with sorrow and don't even know what would make them happy.

It's time to burn the trash. Not tomorrow. Not a week from now. Burn the trash today. Figure out what it is that you need to clean up in your life and clean it up, get rid of it, burn it up. Stop hoarding things that are terrible for you, because they will be your spiritual downfall.

It doesn't just end at burning the things we are holding on to. We have to resort to some more extreme levels. You need to burn the things you know are going to weaken your walls to the point of crumbling. I love how Jesus described this idea because it's so simple that it's almost complicated: *"If your right eye causes you to sin, tear it out and throw it away. For it is better that you lose one of your members than that your whole body be thrown into hell. And if your right hand causes you to sin, cut it off and throw it away. For it is better that you lose one of your members than that your whole body go into hell."* (Matthew 5:29-30). Jesus' solution was fairly simple when it came to temptations that were causing harm: get rid of them. While cutting our arms off and pulling out our eyeballs is merely metaphorical, what Jesus is essentially saying is, "burn the trash". If a computer makes you stumble, get rid of it as much as you can, write on paper instead, only use it when supervised. If you know that a certain person gives you thoughts of doing something you shouldn't, find a new friend, or limit your interaction. If you know that watching a particular show is influencing you poorly, stop watching it.

It's not rocket science, but it is painful beyond all doubt. After we had kids, my wife and I discovered we had accumulated a large collection of movies over the years. One day, one of my kids pulled a movie out and asked to watch it. I was horrified. There was no way my 3 year old was going to be able to watch that. It was that day, we decided we needed to burn some trash. We had to get rid of some stuff that, frankly, we had enjoyed, but it wasn't helping our spiritual lives. Don't get me wrong, we aren't the kind of people who are complete sticks-in-the-mud when it comes to entertainment; but, let's face it, there are some things that Christians just shouldn't be a part of, not matter how fun they are.

Proceed with Caution

I will give you a moderate warning about spiritual trash-burning and rubble-clearing. It almost always leads to discovering things you'd forgotten about. Sometimes, it's good; like finding money in a pair of jeans. You rejoice and your day becomes awesome. However, sometimes you don't find money in old clothes, but a piece of chocolate you were saving for later that has melted all over the back pocket and is now on your hand.

This same thing happens in our spiritual lives. Sometimes, when we remove the rubble, we discover that we had something joyful that we had forgotten about buried beneath it all. We love finding those things because they give us hope to move forward in our quest. Often, though, what we find are painful scars of things we did or said. Things we'd long hoped were gone and forgotten about, but the crater is still there, just waiting to remind us of our humanity. Do not be diverted from your task by this; we will deal with the scars later. Just be warned they are there. Let's clear the rubble. Let's burn the trash. Let's begin a new slate for rebuilding our spiritual walls.

5

Team

Sixth grade was the last year that I ever played basketball. I still remember it like it was yesterday. I was average at most sports. I wasn't going pro, but in sixth grade I decided that I would continue in the "buddy ball" system, rather than join the 5th/6th grade school team. All of the really good players went to the school team and, therefore, if you still played in their system by the time you were in 6th grade, you were generally the best kid out there. I was confident that this would be the case. I was sure to have sheer basketball dominance, the way only Shaquille O'Neal did in his prime. All the other teams were sure to employ a hack-a-ben method in order to contain my awesome skills. In some ways, it was very true. I dominated 4th graders like it was nothing, and at one point scored 24 points in a commanding personal career best game. It would have been glorious, had it not been for the fact that our team lost every game. Every. Single. Game.

My team was comprised of really young talent, some of whom went on to do some pretty great things in athletics, but not at that point. Though, personally I did amazing, as a team - we stunk. Looking back, it was my fault. My arrogance had put us in a position that I felt I could carry us in every game, alone. I couldn't, but it didn't seem like my team could, either. So, I put the team on my back and tried to carry them. But that's not how teamwork operates. You may have a star, but they have to have a supporting cast in order to win. They have to play together to win together.

This concept is one of the ways we fail most in the church today and in Christianity as a whole. When Christianity itself is divided, how can we expect anyone to unite for our cause? Further, I want to make sure you hear what I am about to say: you cannot rebuild your spiritual walls alone. It is impossible. You will fail. You need a team.

The Island of Misfit Toys

Do you remember the scene from the stop-motion animation movie, "Rudolph the Red-nosed Reindeer"? My favorite scene is when Rudolph, Hermie, and Yukon Cornelius travel to the land of misfit toys. Upon arrival, they meet the sentry of the Island, a jack-in-the-box, named Charlie. When Charlie pops out of the box, he says, "Halt, who goes there?"; to which Yukon Cornelius replies, "Us, of course!". Charlie says, "Well, ok then." Charlie goes on to explain that they are on the Island of Misfit Toys, for which he is the official sentry. He's there because he's a jack-in-the box not named Jack.

This scene speaks volumes to me every time I see it. It is a constant reminder of myself and the church at large. I've often tried to be a "jack-in-the-box, named Charlie". I've wanted to be something or do something that I simply didn't have the skills to do. It seems that our lives are often consistent of a band of misfit people. We don't really belong, we don't know what we are good at, so we band together in the one thing that unites us; we're all misfits. It's a funny and powerful image.

The interesting part is that is exactly the scene I see unfold in Nehemiah chapter 3. In the previous chapter, in verse 18, Nehemiah tells the people, "*Let us rise up and build*". Such a great choice of words. He could have said, "I'm gonna rebuild the walls, you guys can come help if you want" but he didn't. He strongly affirmed they were going to do this together. Chapter 3 of Nehemiah is one of those that people often skip because it's pretty much nothing but names. It's not as dry as the genealogies that we usually skip, but it's close. It essentially tells all the people who worked together to begin rebuilding the wall. Just by a rough count of chapter 3, there are more than 30 individuals or groups listed as either building or repairing the walls, gates, and towers. This would be amazing in and of itself, if they were all of the same background or if they were all expert builders with 30 years of building experience, but they weren't. As you read through the text, you'll find they're essentially a band of misfit toys. They weren't people who would normally be together. You have high priests building with goldsmiths, perfumers, and ordinary dudes all with really only one thing in common. They had the same end in mind.

You need these people in your life, even though they don't seem like they fit. You need a team to help you rebuild your walls. Your team needs to consist of people with skill sets that are different from your own. You need people, reliable, Godly people, who will drop their differences and unite with you to help you fortify your soul. You will be the one who has to unite them together and keep them together, but you absolutely need people who love you to do this. These people will come from all walks of life, but they can be united in their goal to get to Heaven and to help you get there, too.

The "I" in Team

I'm not sure who invented the phrase, "there's no 'I' in team", but I would like to know, so I could hug them and high five them in the face with a chair. It's true. I have a love/hate relationship with this, so much so that it irks my soul. On the surface, I love the principle of it; or I would if people took it the way that they should. I've often wanted to say this to many individuals in the church, in hopes they would catch my drift. I've needed it said to me more times than anyone else, but this is not the cause of my hatred for it. My loathsome side for this phrase comes from the fact that I think we have often used it to defer accountability and responsibility to others instead of ourselves.

There is no "I" in team, but there should be. I don't mean that in a selfish way, I just wish everyone on the planet understood that they have a responsibility to themselves. Jesus said that the greatest commandment was to love God with all of yourself, (Matthew 22:36-40). We've nailed that part down. The second command trips us up a bit because it's counter-intuitive to everything that we are taught about love and Christianity. Jesus said the second greatest commandment was to "*love your neighbor as yourself*". It's an odd phrase, summed up nicely by Brian Berry, in his book, *As For Me and*

My Crazy House:

> "But the little phrase that jumped out at me comes
> near the very end—the two words *as yourself*. I'd
> never thought about it much, but as I did, I almost
> thought it was wrong. Maybe Jesus blew it or maybe
> Mark recorded it wrong. Jesus ended by saying we
> should love others like we love ourselves? Really?
> Perhaps it should say, "Love others like you want
> to be loved." Or maybe it should say, "Love others
> selflessly like those who truly love you." Or surely it
> should read, "Love others as God has loved you."
> But none of those are the model Jesus chose to use
> in this summary of God's commands. He didn't even
> use himself in this instance and say, "Love others as
> I have loved you." Instead he said to love others like
> you love yourself."

Brian uses the example of an airline attendant en-
couraging you to put your oxygen mask on before your child's
and, at first, this seems insane, but the reality is that you're
useless to the child if you're dead. Thus, you can never love
your neighbor properly unless you love yourself properly.
That means that we have to take care of ourselves spiritually
first; we must help ourselves before we help anyone else. It's
what keeps us healthy, but also keeps us from being hypo-
critical (Matthew 7:1-2). So, yes, I am suggesting you be a bit
selfish, to a point. You're useless to anyone else if you're dead
spiritually. The beauty of the second greatest commandment
is that it makes us accountable for our neighbor, but also for
ourselves.

I sometimes cringe when I hear people say the phrase,
"I've turned it all over to God". Not always; some cases that

I have seen are so bad, that this is actually a really appropriate response. On the surface, it seems innocent, maybe even a good phrase you would find on a card or one of those motivational pictures with a really neat scenic view of an ocean and awesome typography. But deep down, I think it's not that innocent. It's like we're saying, "I know I got myself into this mess, but I'm just gonna let God clean it up." It usually doesn't work. There's no verse that I know of that says, "If you get to this point in your Christian walk, just give up and God will take care of the rest." It's just the opposite, in fact. God always expects you to play a part in this. You are never without responsibility or accountability, regardless of who's on your team.

Don't be lulled into thinking that just because you have a team of people that are willing to help you do this, that you have less work to do, because you don't. In the end, everything you do is up to you. Nehemiah doesn't just sit back and watch everyone else work. He gets involved, he's active. He didn't even ask God to send down some miracle so they could be home sleeping in their own beds that night. He knew everyone had to be responsible for their part or it would all fail. You are responsible for you. The world owes you nothing and neither does God, but He's willing to give you everything; in fact, He already has. What will you do with it?

Learning to Let Go
I'm a recovering control freak. Of all the things that have irked me in my life, this has been one of the most difficult and devastating aspects of who I am. I like to be in control and when I'm not, I feel very much out of sorts. I'm a terrible backseat driver, which is horrible because I also hate to drive, almost as much as I hate to sit while someone else

drives. It makes me anxious to even think about someone else having control over even the smallest aspect of my life and, frankly, at certain points, it has killed my ministry on so many levels.

For my first few years of ministry, I really felt like I had something to prove, mostly to myself. I wanted to be the guy that got credit for everything, and in order to get the credit, I said "yes" to everything. Because I said "yes" to everything, I had tons to do, but because my motives weren't what they should be, I tried to do everything myself. No matter the event, I was the one that would set it up, decorate it, advertise it, plan it, tear it down, and run it. Most of the things I planned were poorly executed, even though we had fun. Along the way, though, I learned a very important and humbling lesson: I wasn't good at everything. That actually kind of hurt to type. I've never been arrogant about many things, but in my mind, I guess I always thought I could do most anything. I couldn't be more wrong.

What I've learned lately is that there are people who excel at things that I stink at. People who have skill sets that compliment mine and that, often, I am jealous of. My job, now, is to get all of those different skill sets to work together for a common cause. It's a thought that we often lose sight of in the church, but we are all on the same team. Let's act like it.

When I began to understand that other people's talents were different from mine, not better, I began to see my ministry in a whole new fashion. It's the same concept that Paul used in 1 Corinthians 12-14, in conjunction with miraculous spiritual gifts. He had to make them understand they were all part of the same body and that each part had a different, but important, function. In order for the body to function properly, each part has to embrace the job that they have been given. In essence, there's no room for control freaks, each part has to learn to let go.

For all of you fellow control freaks reading this, take a deep breath for what I'm about to say next. It's okay to let go. In fact, it's good and healthy. You need to let go because, in order to rebuild your spiritual walls, it's going to require putting some trust in other people. It's going to take you depending on others who you know you can count on.

Trust is hard, especially if that trust has been violated on any level; it can be very difficult to trust again. Trust takes courage or, at least, it should. There are certain things that everyone is willing to share without hesitation, but there are other things that we aren't sure we would ever trust someone else to know. Case in point, very few times do we hear people willing to admit to soul-crushing mistakes in public, though we are called to confess our sins to one another. The reason, in all honesty, is that we don't trust each other enough. It's not just that we are afraid of what people will think, we honestly conclude that if we confess such things, no one would love us. We would lose their respect, maybe their friendship, but we desperately want to be loved and we will do anything to protect it. The fact is, cliche´ as it may sound, we have always been loved. It's just that God's love never seems to be "enough" for anyone, even though God literally couldn't do anything else to demonstrate His love toward us.

In this wall-building journey, we have to learn to let go. We have to learn to let others help carry our burdens, to trust them enough to let them know where we are in our process, to love them enough to let them use their talents for the glory of The Lord. It's time to let go.

Being Picked Last

I'm not sure that there is anything more shameful than being picked last for something when you were in grade school. It's humiliating. The last pick is always the mercy pick, the kid that was chosen just because the teachers told you everyone had to play. Being picked last stunk, but being the one who picked was awesome. The really cool part about this process is you get to pick who helps you rebuild the walls.

You get to choose the cream of the crop if you want. You get to handpick those who will help you fortify your spiritual life. Choose wisely. Make sure you choose people who have your best interest at heart and not their own. Make sure they are people who follow God explicitly and at all cost. Make sure they are people who never waver from the truth and won't let you, either. Make sure you pick people who will be honest about your successes and your failures. Pick your team and build your walls.

6

Construction

My mom loves to renovate things. I'm not sure we ever lived in a house that she didn't gut the kitchen and redo it. She did a fabulous job, too. I am currently the benefactor of such a kitchen in a house that my parents once owned. Growing up, it was not uncommon for my house to reek of construction work. I'm not sure how to describe that smell, but it is distinct. It was always a very exciting time when the construction was happening and, even though we generally knew what was taking place, the final result was really cool to see.

We have spent the previous chapters doing all the planning and preparation that needed to be done in order to start construction. Today is the day that we begin to reconstruct your spiritual walls. Perhaps, though, you have read this book and thought, "my walls aren't that bad." That's ok; we can still strengthen them even more. Let's start building.

52 Days

Nehemiah completes construction of the city walls in just 52 days. It's an amazing accomplishment beyond words and there is a reason that we continue to talk about this story today. If God can build a city wall in 52 days, imagine what He can do with you.

I don't want you to get the wrong idea here. The process of rebuilding your spiritual walls is not something I can logically put a time frame on. It may take you 5 days, or 100 days to really put your life back in shape, but I know two things are imperative: 1. Make sure your soul is clean today, don't wait; 2. Set a time frame for Spiritual Fortification and keep it. On the latter, I say this with much experience. I can't tell you how many people I hear say things like, "We want to come back to church someday." Guess what? "someday" never comes. Unless you make spiritual fortification a priority and give it the time it needs, you will never complete this goal. Spiritual walls are never truly something you can just be content with. It will take a lifetime commitment to maintaining them, or else you will end up in the same shape you started.

Foundation Is Key

I have made an assumption in this book that I'm not sure I have verbalized thus far; that is, I'm assuming you have need to rebuild your spiritual walls in some capacity or another. That implies that you once had walls, or in the very least, were/are a New Testament Christian. If that's not the case, you need to do that asap, (for the "how", check the following verse: Acts 2:38). Regardless of the state of your walls, in any building project, there isn't a single builder who wouldn't stress the importance of a solid foundation to build on. It doesn't matter how beautiful the structure, if the foundation isn't correct, the rest of it is doomed. This logic applies to spiritual walls, as well.

I run into to people who are tired of hearing about the idea of the basics of Christianity. People who talk of going "deeper", becoming more "spiritual". Those are all noble desires. However, you can't move on to deeper things without establishing a firm, solid foundation on which everything else will be built. Paul said, in 1 Corinthians 3:11, *"For no one can lay a foundation other than that which is laid, which is Jesus Christ."* Every single aspect of our life should be laid against the foundation of Christ. It should be built on Him. This will determine how we think, act, react, live, sleep, and breathe. Every decision we make, with Christ as our foundation, should be held up by Christ. He is our support and the rest of our lives are built on Him.

If you don't truly believe Jesus Christ was who He said He was, your belief is worthless. If you believe Jesus was the Son of God because your parents told you and not because you actually, sincerely believe He was real, then you don't have a foundation at all. The whole concept of belief and all of Christianity is worthless if Christ didn't exist. It's even more worthless if we pseudo-believe that He did. When we truly begin to understand the magnitude of Christ, it will cause us to live so differently that it might just scare us.

The neat part is that you can reliably build upon Him, knowing that this foundation has endured the test of time. For thousands of years, people have built their lives on Jesus and continue to do so today. Every brick that we lay in our spiritual walls will be directly influenced by our foundation. We need the basics to be able to build a stronger, better wall.

Convicted

I occasionally get asked about the so called "youth migration"; it's the "epidemic" that is plaguing the church with somewhere between 50% and 70% of high school kids leaving their faith in college. The question I am usually asked is, "Why do you think so many kids are leaving the church?" A lot of discussion could come into this, but my answer usually boils down to one word: conviction.

It's not just teenagers, either. I believe, in some manner or another, those who choose to live outside of Christ have the roots of their behavior in a lack of conviction. It's almost like spiritual apathy, we have just simply believed what previous generations have taught us. We believe things, not because we truly believe that's what's right, but because we think our parents, grandparents, and friends couldn't be wrong. So, most of the time we adopt a belief similar to what we were taught growing up. Don't get me wrong, this isn't always a bad thing, as long as we are taught to own that belief with all our might.

I've been teaching teen classes long enough to know when I get "church answers" in a class. What I mean is, programmed responses to questions that these kids have been taught over the years. Are they correct answers? Usually. That's not the issue, though. The issue is when you begin to poke and prod deeper. To ask questions about why they believe, for which you almost always receive a response of, "because the Bible says so". So, you poke and prod further. Get them to name book, chapter, and verse, ask questions about context and test them to see if they really believe what they've been taught.

Please, don't fall into this way of thinking. Just because you've been taught something doesn't mean you believe. It doesn't mean it for you or your family. I'm convinced that Nehemiah and his team of misfits were able to rebuild the wall so quickly because they were convicted of what it was that they were doing; or, as Nehemiah put it, *"the people had a mind to work"* (Nehemiah 4:6). They all knew exactly what they wanted to achieve and weren't going to let anyone convince them otherwise.

As we are building our spiritual walls, we must be convicted about our beliefs. We must know exactly what we believe and take a stand for it. We must build these beliefs on the foundation of Jesus Christ and we must truly believe in them. So how do you properly develop conviction?

1. Pray about it. It's sad that something so powerful has been cliched enough that it no longer sounds powerful. As a Christian, you have access to an almighty God; use Him. Pray for Him to soften your heart, pray for Him to give you understanding. This is absolutely the place to start.

2. Study the Word of God. Notice, I didn't say "read". Reading is good, but studying develops conviction. Study with the desire to see what God truly wants, not what someone is telling you He wants. All of our convictions must be based on the inerrant Word of God (2 Tim 3: 16-17). If our convictions are based on anything else, they will fail to uphold in times of need. Study the Word, know what you believe, and why you believe it. Be ready to defend it against all attacks. Start with the basics and work your way up.

Gates, Doors, and Bolts

So, maybe you have a firm foundation and a strong conviction of your beliefs, but your walls are still torn down. Don't be discouraged. We can rebuild them using some of the prep work that we have done in this book. As you read Nehemiah chapter 3 again, I want you to notice something besides the names; I want you to notice what these people were building. Almost all of them are rebuilding gates.

A few chapters ago, we discussed the idea of removing rubble, and I told you to identify your weak spots, to remember the weakest spots in your spiritual walls and the things you struggle with most. Then I asked you to make sure you rid yourself of the trash. Hopefully, at this point, you have done that. If you haven't yet, now would be a good time to do so.

Removing the rubble and identifying weak spots is a good thing to do and a great place to start, but contrary to popular belief, removing sin is not the end of your work. True repentance involves, not just sorrow and stopping an action, but remorse and replacement of old actions with another. When Nehemiah cleared the rubble from the wall, he had to replace it with something better, something that ensured it would last. We need to do those things.

Much of Christianity isn't about removing bad things or not doing bad things though, it is a part of it, and the part that often gets the most attention. We don't serve under a "sin management" lifestyle, so to speak. I'm a firm believer this is why so many today do not have spiritual fortification worth anything. We've focused so long on removing bad stuff, but never replaced it with good stuff.

When Jesus was giving the sermon on the mount, He said things like, *"You have heard it said you shall love your neighbor and hate your enemy. But I say to you, love your enemies and pray for*

those who persecute you," (Matthew 5:43-44). Notice, Jesus starts
with something that obviously isn't good. Loving your neighbor is great, hating your enemy is common, but not good.
Jesus' commandment doesn't just say, "don't hate your enemy". Instead of simply removing the behavior, Jesus commands that we replace the behavior with something entirely
more effective; not just to love them, but love and pray for
them. Why? Because replacing negative behavior and leaving
it alone creates a void that will eventually be filled with more
negative behavior. However, replacing the negative behavior
with something positive doesn't leave as much room for the
negative behavior to seep back in.

In rebuilding our spiritual walls, let's take our weak
points and replace them with godly, holy actions and thinking. Particularly, we need to change the way that we think. So
often, we think of sin in terms of actions. "I did this or that",
but the reality is that all sins are first mental. If Satan wins the
battle for my mind, he will eventually win the battle for my
actions. So, in order to better spiritually fortify ourselves, we
must learn to rethink how we look at the world. That means
we have to dwell on different things than we did before.

Paul put this concept beautifully when he said, *"Fi-
nally, brothers whatever is true, whatever is honorable, whatever is just,
whatever is lovely, whatever is commendable, if there is any excellence, if
there is anything worthy of praise, think about these things"* (Philippians 4:8). See how Paul didn't say, "just stop thinking of bad
stuff"? No, he encouraged the saints to dwell on good things;
Heavenly things, if you will. If we are going to have spiritual
walls that last, it's going to take changing the way that we
think. Replacing unholy with holy, secular with spiritual.

Let's make this a bit more practical. Let's say that you
struggle with lust, something that is extremely rampant in our

society today. Sex sells and, frankly, it has sold many on the idea. Maybe you're addicted to lust in the form of pornography. Perhaps, for years, you've fought with it. In our preparation for construction, we should have taken the means necessary to diminish this addiction. This would include confiding in someone about the nature of the sin, being accountable to them and yourself, and removing, as best you can, the temptations to fall into the action again. If we stop there, though, this will still and will always be our weak point. We have to replace this behavior with something more positive and more spiritual. So, when you are tempted to engage in this damaging behavior you have an alternative to focus on instead. Maybe it's studying God's Word, or praying, or journaling, or underwater basket-weaving. You must replace the negative with a positive and change the way you think. You must stop looking at people as sex objects alone and begin to see them as souls.

This could apply not just to lust, but all sins and temptations. The strongest walls we can build will be built upon the principle of replacing old blocks with new, better blocks.

Towers

One of the other things you will notice about Nehemiah 3 is not only are they building and repairing gates, but also towers. Towers were key in the defense of a city. They allowed the soldiers to be given a height advantage and, most importantly, vision to see an oncoming attack.

A major problem with our spirituality today is that most of us lack vision. We lack vision to see where we are going and what is coming. Few things are more valuable than being able to see where an attack will be coming from.

71

However, there is also value in having the vision to see where you want to be. This is extremely important in our spiritual fortification

We need to have a vision for where we want to be spiritually. You won't be able to see or plan for every attack but you can be as prepared as possible. Where do you want to be spiritually in 1 month? 1 year? 5 years? What are you doing to achieve those goals? You need towers to be able to see ahead; to see what is coming ahead both the enemy and where you want to go. Have vision. Don't get blind-sided by failing to see forward.

If you have done the prep work, it's time to get your hands dirty with construction. It's far past time that our country, our families took a spiritual stance. We have to draw a firm line in the sand and let no one cross it. Today is the day to put on your hard hat and begin construction. Get to work on those walls!

7

Victory

    I'm the black sheep of my family, and it all has to do with one pivotal moment in sports history. My family are hard-core University of Kentucky basketball fans. I mean, seriously devoted to this. My sweet mother turns into a vicious television-yeller when UK plays. This is the home that I grew up in. In 1992, a guy named Christian Laettner changed my life, though it would take me a few years to realize it. If you've ever watched a single game of the NCAA tourney, you know exactly what I'm talking about. If not, just Google, the shot by Christian Laettner. Needless to say, Duke basketball has never been highly esteemed in the minds of Kentucky fans. I remember the shot, even as a boy; and I became a Duke fan, and remain one to this day. I'm the sports black sheep of my family and my congregation.

It's amazing how one victory can change everything. How many underdogs in sports have had a single victory be something that changes their whole season? Everyone loves to win. No one likes to lose. You need a victory. Although, as we discussed last chapter, it may take years to properly restore your spiritual walls. You should celebrate a victory for even starting the journey.

Critics

Chapter 4 of Nehemiah takes a turn for the worst, in terms of mood. The first couple of chapters show enormous progress, but chapter four shows what happens when people began to succeed. For every victory, you will have someone who doesn't like it. You will never please everyone. You will always have critics.

Nehemiah's critics are pretty harsh. The first verse of Nehemiah 4 says that his critics were greatly enraged and angry. They are positively red with rage over this, so much so that they begin to mock the people regarding their crafts-manship and even ask God not to forgive them of their sins, (that's pretty harsh). Eventually, this talk turns into them plotting to take action to stop Nehemiah and his friends.

I love Nehemiah's reaction to this. The first thing Nehemiah does, in verse 9, is pray to God that He would protect them day and night. The great irony of ironies, isn't it? Nehemiah is building a wall for protection while asking God to build a wall of protection around them. Nehemiah understood the importance of spiritual fortification in order to accomplish what he knew he needed to.

You will have people who will criticize what you are doing. They will be angry at you for changing. They will accuse you of being a hypocrite. They will try to stop you from changing. You must not let them to get to you. You must press forward to victory. Listen to what Nehemiah says to his people in 4:14, "And I looked and arose and said to the nobles and to the officials and to the rest of the people, 'Do not be afraid of them. Remember the Lord, who is great and awesome, and fight for your brothers, your sons, your daughters, your wives, and your homes'." It's time to fight for yourself and for your family! Take a stand!

The people respond to this by building with spears in their hands and watching each other's backs. This is, once again, the importance of a having a team you can trust. Someone to watch your back when you are in trouble and to be able to support you when you are dealing with critics and people who want you to fail.

Since breaking into the world of writing and speaking, I have experienced things I never thought I would; signing copies of books, preaching before hundreds of people, book-stores calling to order our books, and encountering a whole lot of critics. Before I started writing on a regular basis, I remember attending a conference where a very well-known author spoke. When asked what it takes to be a writer, he replied, "You've got to have thick skin." I'm not sure a better answer has ever been given. In everything you do, there will be people who criticize your work. It's a part of life, but I've always struggled with personal criticism.

These are some things that have helped me:

1. You can't please everyone. I've struggled with this for a long time. In my search to make everyone happy, I've learned it is impossible. What pleases one will, inevitably, displease someone else. Recently, I've learned to just try to please God and the rest I won't worry about (Hebrews 12:2). Not everyone is going to love your work, but that doesn't mean your work isn't good or beneficial; it just means you

can't please everyone.

2. Some critiques are correct. This one has always been hard for me to swallow. Sometimes, a critic's assessments of my work have been spot-on and I just failed to accept it. Generally, when people hear something negative about what they have done, their first reaction is to become defensive. I have found that by doing that, I miss an opportunity to make something better (Proverbs 15:32).

3. It's usually not personal. Most of the time, the criticism you receive is about your work, and not you. The person is making a statement about what you have done, not who you are. The problem in that, for me, is being able to separate the two. I may feel that my work defines who I am, but it's simply not true.

4. You're a critic, too. Sometimes I catch myself "commenting" on other people's sermons or writings and realize I am doing the same thing I often hate. Everyone is a critic from time to time, we just don't usually realize it. Criticizing something you weren't a part of is one of the easiest things in the world to do. It is much easier to comment on someone else's work than to do the work yourself. Before you criticize anyone, ask yourself, "Would this be helpful to me if I were in their shoes?"

5. You shouldn't let critics stop you. I've met people who are so afraid of what people think that they never do the things they have the capability of doing. It's probably one of the reasons people fear public speaking. Don't let the fear of being criticized stop you from rebuilding your walls!. Remember, critics are humans, just like you and me.

Being a Christian and being someone who tries to please everyone are not things that have ever gotten along well. Frankly, Christianity will offend some people. Don't be surprised when it happens. If you are living your Christian life properly it will eventually lead to making some people extremely angry when you refuse to compromise your beliefs. Don't give up, build those walls.

Celebration and Victory

"*So the wall was finished on the twenty-fifth day of the month Elul, in fifty-two days. And when all our enemies heard of it, all the nations around us were afraid and fell greatly in their own esteem, for they perceived that this work had been accomplished with the help of our God*" (Nehemiah 6:15-16). Despite everything working against them, they finished what they had started, and in record time. 52 days. I love the second part of that verse. All the nations that surrounded them were afraid because they knew what had happened. They saw the presence of God in their lives. This is quite the contrast for what they were 52 days previously, when Nehemiah called his city a disgrace and shameful. Now they were powerful and fear-inducing. No enemy wanted to mess with them.

Imagine what God can do with you in 52 days if you work hard and let God do His part. He can make you into something you never thought you could be. It will take tears, sweat, and a whole lot of sacrifice, but it is the way to go from shameful to being feared by our spiritual enemies. What a difference a wall can make! Celebrate every victory. Rejoice with each brick. Press on and build your wall! Let's rebuild the spiritual walls of ourselves, our family, and our nation. If we want to change the world, let's start with ourselves.